A note for parents and teachers

This Ladybird *First Dictionary* is an ideal first picture
dictionary for young people learning English.
You can help beginners to get the most out of the
dictionary in a way that makes learning English both
interesting and fun.

More than one hundred and thirty attractive illustrations
of everyday words, each clearly labelled, provide
an easy to remember introduction to the English alphabet
and a first English vocabulary. The detailed pictures
will give you lots to talk about and can form the basis for
sharing enjoyable language games.

The *First Dictionary* also introduces numbers from one to
twenty, the days of the week and the months of
the year in clear, simple designs, with lively illustrations
for easy reading and learning. The reference pages at the
end of this book offer useful additional grammar notes.

The *First Dictionary Workbook* in this new Ladybird series
provides further practice in the use of the alphabet and
the words which have been learned in this book.

Further information on local Ladybird stockists
may be obtained from the International Sales Department
Ladybird Books Ltd Beeches Road Loughborough
Leicestershire LE11 2NQ UK
Telephone: + 44 509 268021   Fax: + 44 509 219158

A catalogue record for this book is available
from the British Library

Published by Ladybird Books Ltd Loughborough Leicestershire UK
Ladybird Books Inc Auburn Maine 04210 USA

Printed in the United Kingdom by Ladybird Books Ltd – Loughborough

First Dictionary

words by Valerie Mendes
pictures by John Lobban

Aa actor

airport

Aa apple

arm

Aa artist

asleep

Bb baby

ball

Bb banana

bed

Bb bicycle

bridge

a b c d e f g h i j k l m

Cc cake

camera

Cc cat

chair

Cc comb

cup

A B C D E F G H I J K L M

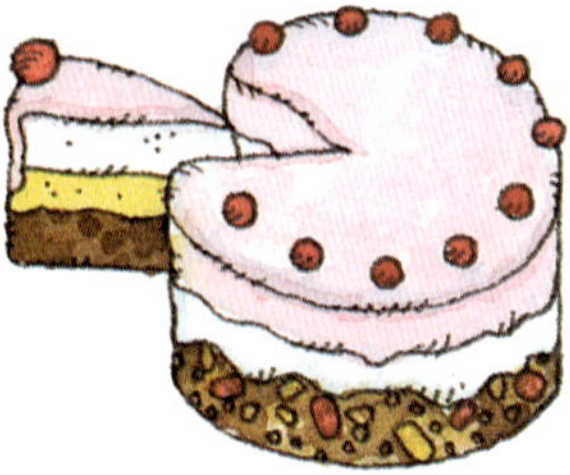

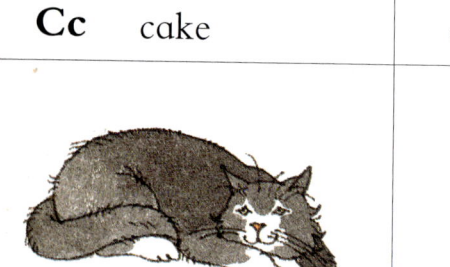

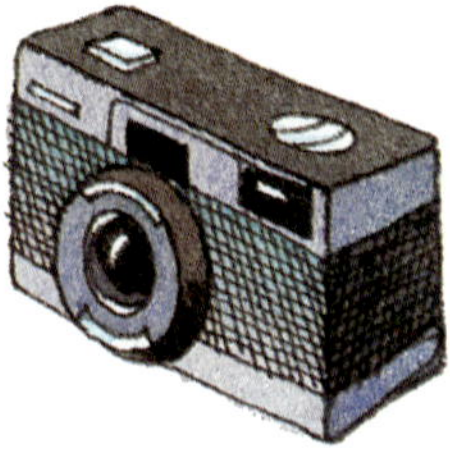

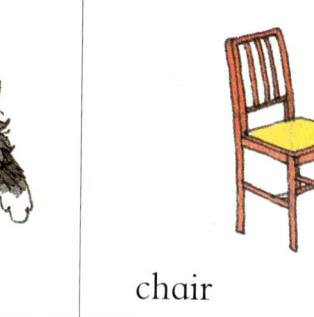

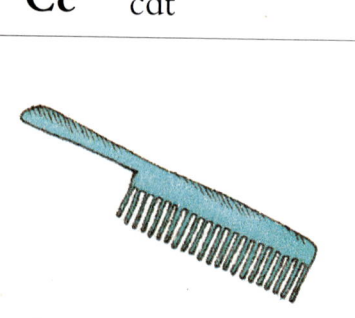

Dd   desk

doctor

Dd   dog

door

Dd   dress

drink

Ee ear

eat

Ee egg

elephant

Ee engine

eye

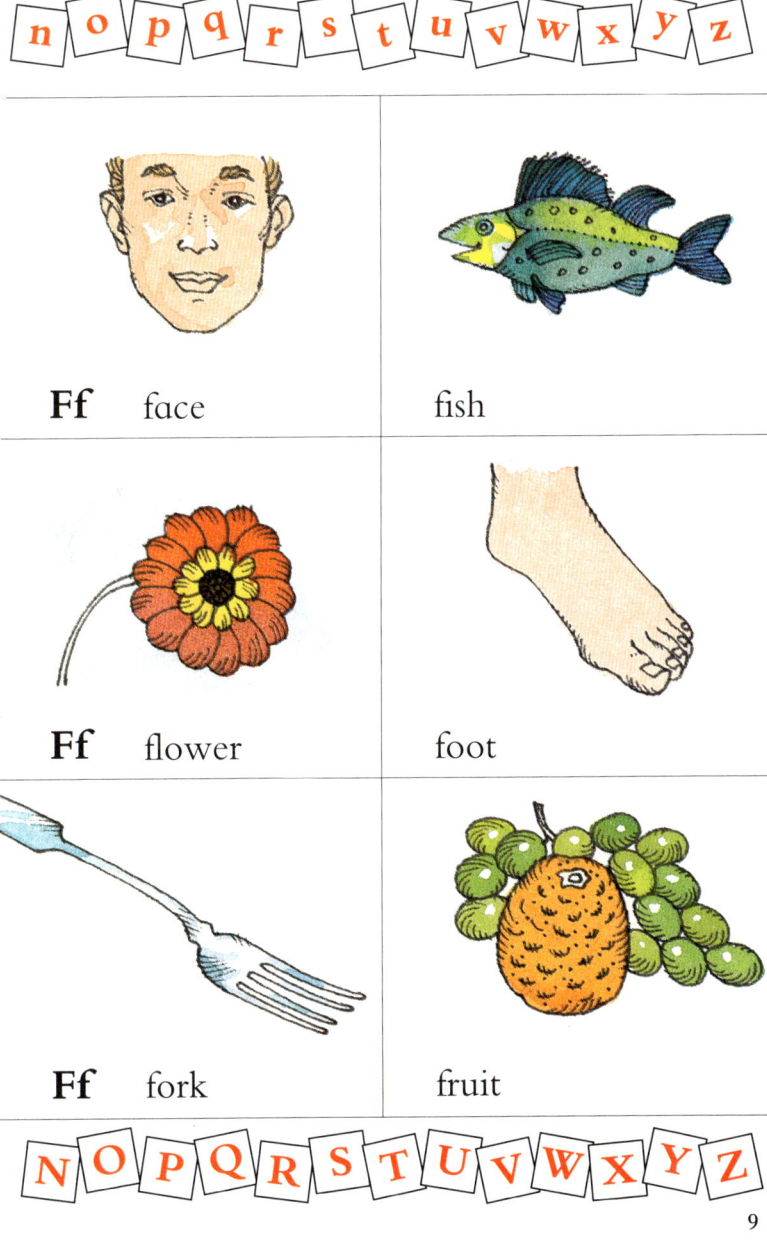

Ff   face

fish

Ff   flower

foot

Ff   fork

fruit

Gg garage

gate

Gg ghost

girl

Gg glass

guitar

Hh hand

hat

Hh hill

horse

Hh hospital

house

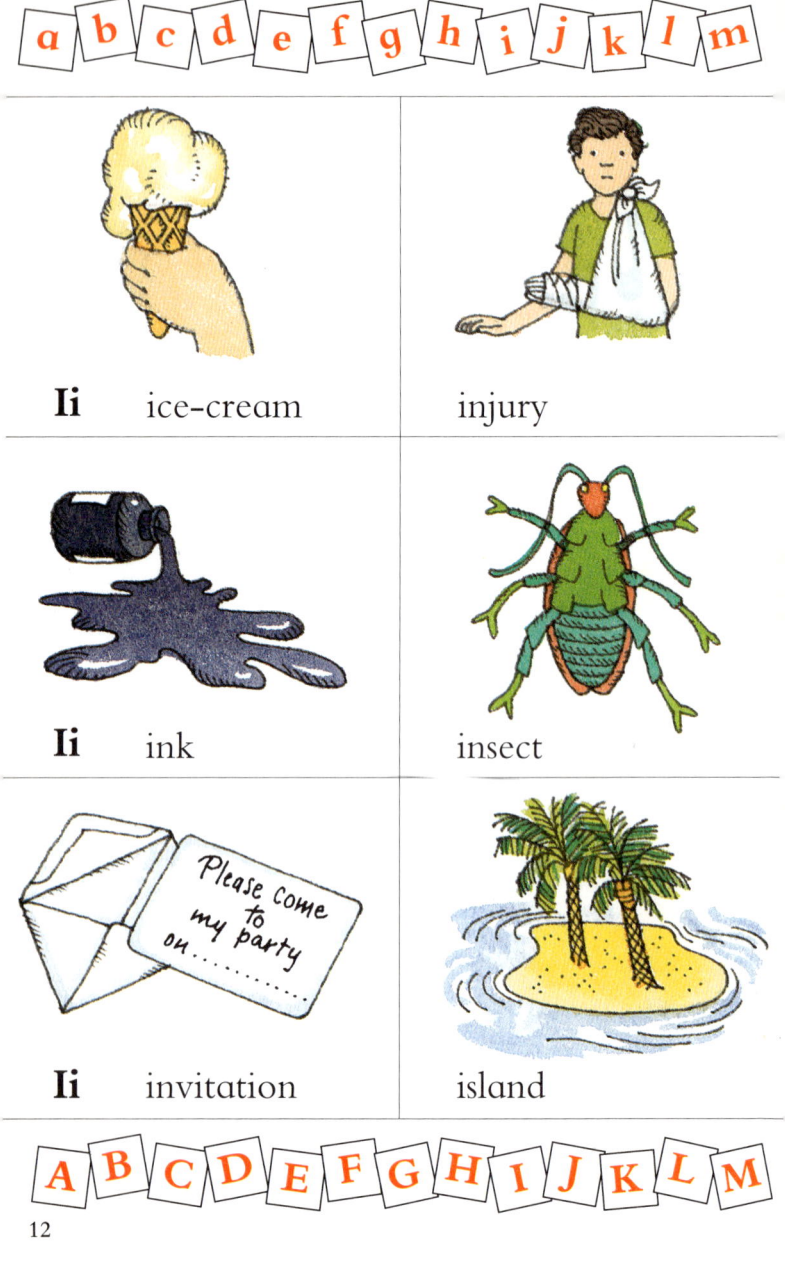

Ii   ice-cream

injury

Ii   ink

insect

Ii   invitation

island

Please come to my party on..........

n o p q r s t u v w x y z

Jj jacket

jar

Jj jazz

jeans

Jj jet

jump

N O P Q R S T U V W X Y Z

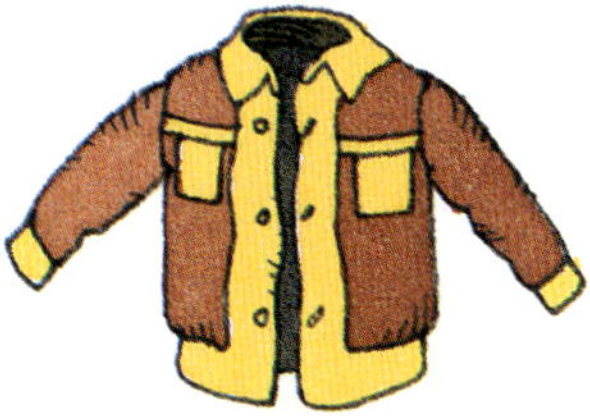

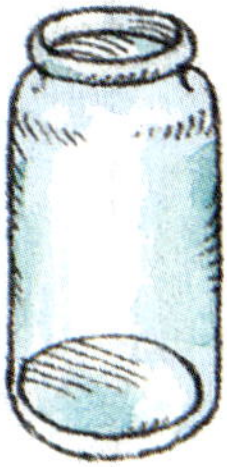

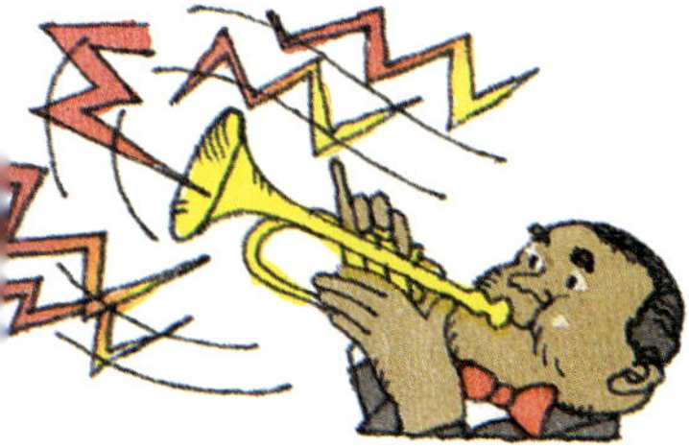

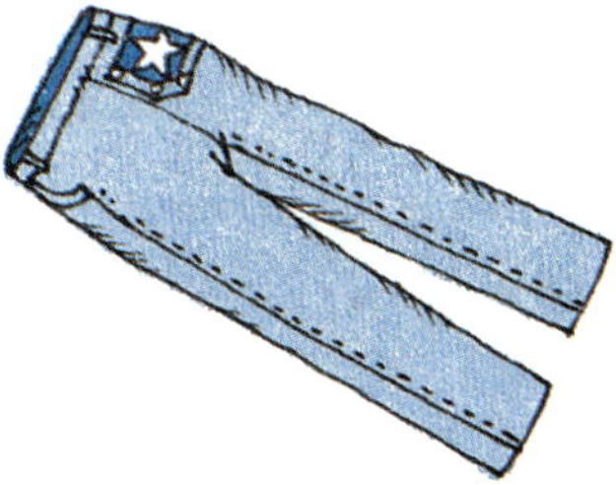

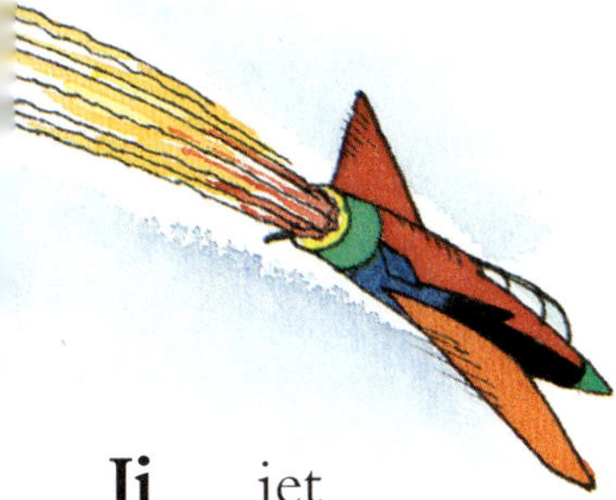

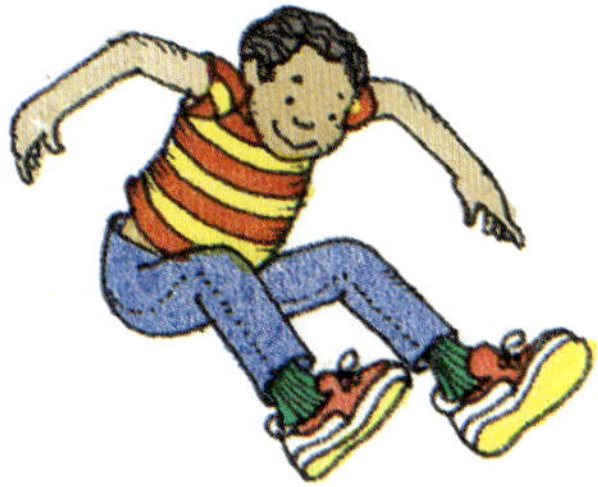

Kk key

kick

Kk king

kiss

Kk kitchen

knife

Ll leaf

leg

Ll letter

library

Ll lion

lunch

Mm   magazine

man

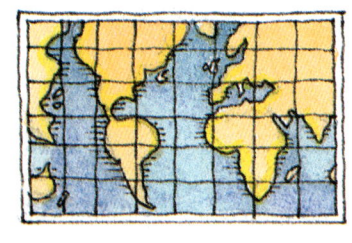

Mm   map

marry

Mm   mirror

mountain

Nn neck

newspaper

Nn night

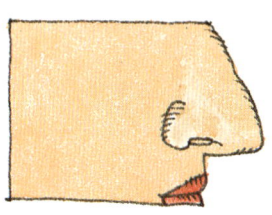

nose

Nn numbers

nurse

Oo   office

old

Oo   orange

Pp   party

Pp   pen

picture

Pp pilot

plate

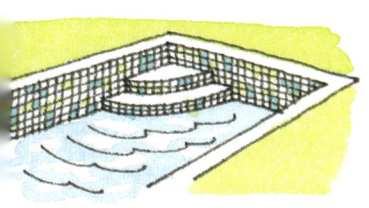

Pp pool

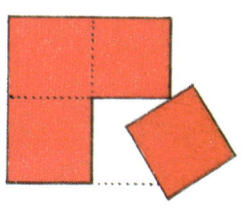

Qq quarter

Qq queen

question

Rr   radio

rain

Rr   rat

river

Rr   roof

rose

Ss ship

shoe

Ss soap

spoon

Ss sun

swim

Tt   table

telephone

Tt   tiger

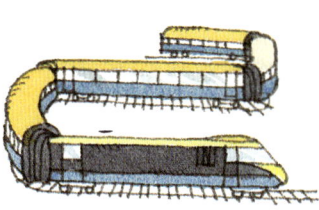

train

Tt   treasure

tree

Uu   umbrella

underground

Uu   upstairs

Vv   valley

Vv   van

volcano

Ww   wash

waterfall

Ww   wheel

window

Ww   woman

write

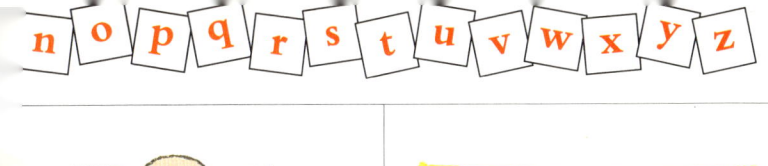

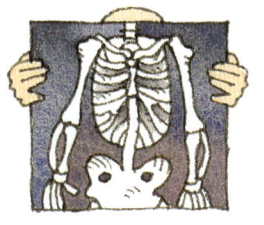

Xx X-ray

Yy yellow

Yy yes

yogurt

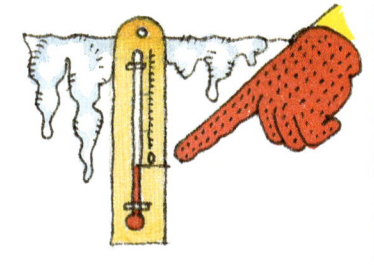

Zz zero

zoo

Numbers one to twenty

one	two	three	four
five	six	seven	eight
nine	ten	eleven	twelve
thirteen	fourteen	fifteen	sixteen
seventeen	eighteen	nineteen	twenty

Days of the week

Monday	Tuesday	Wednesday
Thursday	Friday	Saturday
	Sunday	

Months of the year

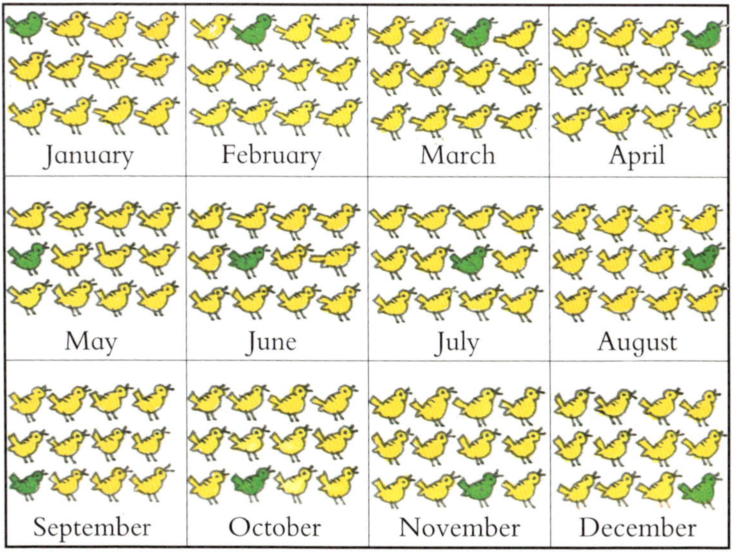

January	February	March	April
May	June	July	August
September	October	November	December

Useful grammar notes

Plurals of some dictionary words

Most nouns in English form their plural by adding the letter *s* – for example: *arm, arms; cat, cats; hand, hands.*

But the following nouns have *irregular* plurals: we form the plurals in a different way. In some cases, the noun remains the same:

Singular	*Plural*
baby	babies
dress	dresses
fish	fish
foot	feet
glass	glasses
injury	injuries
kiss	kisses